*Switzerland Travel Guide 20*_

SWITZERLAND TRAVEL GUIDE 2024-2025

An Atlas Road Map to Zurich, Geneva, Lucerne, Zermatt, Interlaken, Bern, Lausanne, Montreux, St. Moritz, Vevey & Sion

By

JUDE K. BREMNER

Switzerland Travel Guide 2024-2025/Jude K. Bremner

WELCOME TO SWITZERLAND

(Map of Switzerland with Neighborhoods)

Switzerland Travel Guide 2024-2025/Jude K. Bremner

COPYRIGHT

This book written by **Jude K. Bremner** is protected by copyright © 2024. No part of this book may be reproduced, stored, or transmitted in any form or by any means, electronic, mechanical, photocopying, recording or otherwise, without the prior written permission of the copyright owner, except for brief quotations embodied in critical reviews and certain noncommercial uses permitted by copyright law.

DISCLAIMER

The information provided in this eBook, **"SWITZERLAND TRAVEL GUIDE 2024-2025,"** authored by **Jude K. Bremner**, is intended for general informational purposes only. Readers are advised to use the content as a guide.

Legal Compliance

The author and publisher have made efforts to comply with copyright and intellectual property laws. If any inadvertent infringement is identified, it is unintentional, and the author encourages notification for prompt correction.

Conclusion:

"SWITZERLAND TRAVEL GUIDE 2024-2025," is a tool for inspiration and planning, but it does not substitute personalized travel advice or professional consultation. Readers should exercise prudence and diligence in their travel endeavors.

By using this guide, readers acknowledge and accept the terms of this disclaimer. The author and publisher disclaim any liability for outcomes resulting from the use or interpretation of the information provided herein. **Travel safely and enjoy the wonders of Switzerland with an informed and discerning mindset.**

Switzerland Travel Guide 2024-2025/Jude K. Bremner

About The Author

Jude K. Bremner is the person who authored **"SWITZERLAND TRAVEL GUIDE 2024-2025." Jude** loves exploring different cultures and places, and he wants to share his excitement and knowledge with you through this guide.

A Passionate Traveler:

Jude started traveling to understand the unique stories of each place. He's been to bustling cities and Nations, remote landscapes, and hidden spots, all to discover what makes each destination special.

His Love for Switzerland:

Jude's love for **Switzerland** runs deep. Through multiple visits, he has immersed himself in the region's vibrant neighborhoods and pedaled along its scenic canals. **His encounters shape the authentic insights that make this guide an indispensable companion.**

Master of Insider Tips:

Jude is good at finding hidden gems and authentic experiences. **He wants to share these with you so you can have a memorable trip beyond the usual tourist spots.**

Author's Vision:

Jude's vision with this guide is to help you explore Switzerland like a pro. Exploring **Switzerland** like a pro means to dive into **its culture, history, and vibrant atmosphere,** even without experiencing confusion in the long run or being worried about anything.

Let **Jude** be your reliable companion, unveiling the mysteries of **Switzerland** and ensuring your journey transcends mere travel, transforming into **a truly enriching experience.**

Table of Contents

TITLE PAGE

COPYRIGHT

ABOUT THE AUTHOR

TABLE OF CONTENTS

CHAPTER ONE: Introduction to Switzerland
- Overview of Switzerland
  - Geography and Climate
  - Culture and Languages
  - Currency and Practical Tips
- Travel Essentials
  - Visa Information
  - Health and Safety
  - Transportation Options

CHAPTER TWO: Zurich
- Key Attractions
  - Old Town (Altstadt)
  - Bahnhofstrasse
  - Lake Zurich
- Dining and Shopping
  - Local Cuisine
  - Shopping Districts
- Accommodation Recommendations

- Hotels
- Budget Options

CHAPTER THREE: Geneva

- Key Attractions
  - Jet d'Eau
  - United Nations Headquarters
  - Geneva Old Town
- Dining and Shopping
  - Recommended Restaurants
  - Boutique Shopping
- Accommodation Recommendations
  - Hotels
  - Budget Options

CHAPTER FOUR: Lucerne and Lake Lucerne

- Key Attractions
  - Chapel Bridge and Water Tower
  - Lion Monument
  - Lake Cruises
- Dining and Shopping
  - Local Cuisine
  - Shopping in Lucerne
- Accommodation Recommendations
  - Hotels
  - Budget Options

CHAPTER FIVE: Zermatt and the Matterhorn

- Key Attractions

- Matterhorn Glacier Paradise
- Gornergrat Railway
- Hiking Trails

- Dining and Shopping
  - Alpine Dining
  - Specialty Shops
- Accommodation Recommendations
  - Hotels
  - Budget Options

CHAPTER SIX: Interlaken, Bern, Lausanne, Montreux, St. Moritz, Vevey, and Sion

- Interlaken
  - Key Attractions
  - Outdoor Activities
- Bern
  - Historical Sites (Key Attractions)
- Lausanne
  - Museums (Key Attractions)
- Montreux
  - Lakefront and Festivals
- St. Moritz
  - Winter Sports (Key Attractions)
- Vevey
  - Culinary Delights (Key Attractions)
- Sion
  - Historical Sites (Key Attractions)

CHAPTER SEVEN: 7-Day Itinerary

- Day 1: Zurich
    - Morning: Arrival and Old Town Exploration
    - Afternoon: Lake Zurich and Bahnhofstrasse
    - Evening: Dinner and Local Entertainment
- Day 2: Lucerne
    - Morning: Travel to Lucerne and Chapel Bridge
    - Afternoon: Lion Monument and Lake Cruise
    - Evening: Dinner in Lucerne
- Day 3: Interlaken
    - Morning: Travel to Interlaken
    - Afternoon: Outdoor Activities and Lake Views
    - Evening: Relax and Explore Local Dining
- Day 4: Zermatt
    - Morning: Travel to Zermatt
    - Afternoon: Matterhorn Glacier Paradise
    - Evening: Alpine Dining
- Day 5: Geneva
    - Morning: Travel to Geneva
    - Afternoon: Jet d'Eau and UN Headquarters

- Evening: Explore Old Town and Dinner
- Day 6: Bern
  - Morning: Travel to Bern
  - Afternoon: Historical Sites and Bear Park
  - Evening: Local Cuisine
- Day 7: Lausanne and Montreux
  - Morning: Travel to Lausanne
  - Afternoon: Explore Lausanne and Travel to Montreux
  - Evening: Lakefront Stroll and Farewell Dinner

OTHER BOOKS RECOMMENDATION

A KIND GESTURE

Switzerland Travel Guide 2024-2025/Jude K. Bremner

Switzerland Travel Guide 2024-2025/Jude K. Bremner

Chapter One: Introduction to Switzerland

Geography and Climate (Overview of Switzerland)

Geographically, this beautiful and amazing Country is bounded by other Countries of great interest. Those countries are Germany, France, Italy, and Austria. Switzerland has a natural beauty that is unexplainable! The Swiss Alps cover a big part of Switzerland, making it a popular place for skiing and hiking. Besides mountains, there are many lakes, like Lake Geneva and Lake Zurich, which are great for boat rides and picnics.

The weather in Switzerland can change a lot. In the summer, the weather is usually warm and perfect for outdoor activities. Winter brings snow, especially in the mountains, making it a great time for skiing and snowboarding. Spring and autumn are mild and can be a good time to enjoy nature without the crowds.

Culture and Languages

Switzerland has a rich culture with a mix of influences from nearby countries. People in Switzerland speak four main languages: German, French, Italian, and Romansh. This means you will hear different languages as you travel around the country. Each region has its own unique culture and traditions, adding to the charm of Switzerland.

Swiss people are known for being polite and helpful. They take great care of their country, and you'll see this in the clean streets and well-maintained parks. Switzerland is also famous for its delicious chocolate, cheese, and watches.

Currency and Practical Tips

The currency used in this amazing Country is the Swiss Franc (CHF). Yes! Even though Switzerland is part of Europe, it doesn't use the Euro. It's a good idea to have some Swiss Francs with you, but many places also accept credit cards.

When traveling in Switzerland, you'll find that trains, buses, and boats are excellent ways to get around. The Swiss public transportation system is very reliable and easy to use. If you're planning to visit several places, you might want to look into a Swiss Travel Pass, which offers unlimited travel on public transportation for a certain number of days.

Swiss people value punctuality, so it's important to be on time for appointments and public transportation. Also, Switzerland is a very safe country, but like anywhere, it's good to stay alert and take basic safety precautions.

Visa Information (Travel Essentials)

If you're planning to visit Switzerland, you might need a visa depending on where you come from. A visa is a special permit that allows you to enter and stay in a country.

For most people from countries in the European Union (EU) or the Schengen Area, a visa is not needed for short trips. However, if you come from a country outside these areas, you might need to apply for a Schengen visa.

To get a visa, you usually need to fill out an application form, provide a passport photo, and show proof of travel insurance and accommodation. It's a good idea to check with the Swiss embassy or consulate in your country for the most up-to-date information before you travel.

Health and Safety

Switzerland is known for being a very safe country with excellent healthcare facilities. However, it's still important to be prepared. Make sure you have health insurance that covers you while you're abroad. If you need to see a doctor or go to a hospital, Switzerland has high-quality medical services.

While Switzerland doesn't have specific health risks, it's always good to be up-to-date on routine vaccines. Also, make sure to carry any necessary medications with you and have a copy of your prescription just in case.

In terms of safety, Switzerland is one of the safest countries in the world. Violent crime is rare, but it's still wise to be careful with your belongings, especially in busy places like train stations and tourist spots.

Transportation Options

Getting around Switzerland is easy and convenient. The country has a well-organized public transportation system that includes trains, buses, and boats.

- Trains

Trains are a popular way to travel in Switzerland. They are comfortable and connect almost every part of the country. The Swiss Federal Railways (SBB) operates most of the trains, and you can buy tickets at stations or online. Trains run frequently, so you can plan your trip without much hassle.

- Buses

Buses are great for reaching places that are not accessible by train. They cover areas that might not have a train station and are also useful for traveling within cities. Bus schedules are usually available at local transit stations or online.

- Boats

Switzerland has several beautiful lakes, and taking a boat ride is a wonderful way to see the scenery. Regular boat services operate on lakes like Lake Geneva, Lake Zurich, and Lake Lucerne. They can be a relaxing way to travel between towns and enjoy the stunning views.

- Cars

If this is your preference, then you may need to consider renting a car for your usage. Just remember that driving in the Swiss Alps can be challenging in winter due to snow and ice, so make sure your vehicle is equipped for such conditions.

- Bicycles

In many cities and towns, you can rent bicycles to explore the area. Switzerland is bike-friendly, and you'll find dedicated bike paths and trails, especially in scenic regions.

Switzerland's public transportation is known for being punctual and efficient, making it easy for travelers to get around. Whether you choose to take the train, bus, boat, or rent a car, you'll find that getting from one place to another is straightforward and enjoyable.

Chapter Two: Zurich

Old Town -Altstadt (Key Attractions)

This famous location in Zurich is known as it's historical heart. It's like walking back in time! The streets are narrow and winding, and many of the buildings are very old. When you visit the Old Town, you can see colorful houses, ancient churches, and charming squares.

One of the highlights in Altstadt is the Grossmünster Church. This church is really old and has two tall towers that you can see from far away. Another important spot is the Fraumünster Church, which is famous for its beautiful stained glass windows made by the artist Marc Chagall.

Walking around the Old Town, you will find lots of small shops and cafes. You can enjoy a snack or buy a souvenir while you explore.

The Old Town is also home to the Rathaus, which is Zurich's old town hall, and it's a lovely building to check out.

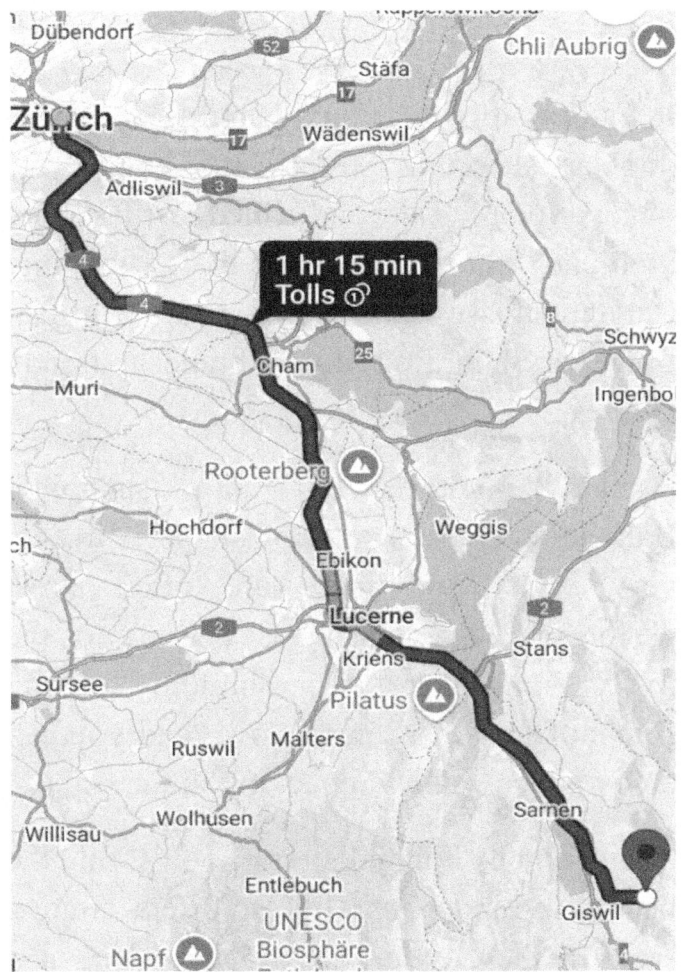

- The map above shows distance (with time covered) from Switzerland central area/location to Zurich

Bahnhofstrasse

In Zurich, this location or area is one of its popular shopping streets. It's known for being very clean and lined with many high-end shops. If you like shopping, Bahnhofstrasse is the place to be. You can find everything from luxury brands to trendy clothes.

Even if you're not into shopping, Bahnhofstrasse is worth a visit. The street is very wide, and there are often street performers and musicians adding to the lively atmosphere. The buildings along Bahnhofstrasse are impressive, and you can enjoy a nice walk while taking in the sights.

At the end of Bahnhofstrasse, you'll find the beautiful Lindenhof Hill. It offers a great view of the city and the river, making it a perfect spot for taking photos.

Lake Zurich

Lake Zurich is a large lake that is right in the heart of the city. The lake is surrounded by parks and paths where you can go for a walk or have a picnic.

One of the best things to do at Lake Zurich is to take a boat ride. You can hop on a boat and enjoy a peaceful trip on the lake while admiring the city's skyline and the surrounding mountains. There are also lots of swans and ducks around the lake, which are fun to watch.

If you prefer staying on land, you can walk or cycle along the lake's promenade. There are many cafes and restaurants where you can sit and enjoy the view. The lake is especially beautiful at sunset when the sky changes colors and reflects on the water.

In the summer, Lake Zurich becomes a popular spot for swimming. There are areas where you can swim safely and enjoy the cool water.

Local Cuisine (Dining and Shopping)

Swiss food is tasty and has many special dishes that you should try when you're in Zurich. Here are some popular Swiss foods:

- Fondue

This is a famous Swiss dish where you melt cheese in a pot and dip pieces of bread into it. It's fun to eat and very yummy. Some places also make fondue with chocolate for dessert.

- Rösti

Rösti is like a big, crispy potato pancake. It's usually served with other dishes like meat or eggs and is a great side dish.

- Raclette

This dish involves melting cheese and scraping it over boiled potatoes, pickles, and vegetables. It's warm and comforting, perfect for a chilly day.

- Swiss Chocolate

Switzerland is known for its chocolate, and there are many brands and flavors to try.

You can find everything from milk chocolate to rich dark chocolate.

- Swiss Pastries

Try some Swiss pastries like buttery croissants or sweet, soft cakes. They are often served in cafes and make a great treat with a hot drink.

Shopping Districts

Zurich has several shopping areas where you can find everything from fancy shops to cool local stores. If you planned to go shopping in Zurich, consider these options or places:

- Bahnhofstrasse

Just like as I have already emphasized, this area is a perfect place to go for your shopping. It has lots of high-end stores where you can buy clothes, shoes, and accessories. Even if you're not buying anything, it's fun to walk along the street and look at the displays.

- Altstadt (Old Town)

In the Old Town, you'll find lots of small, unique shops. This area is great for finding special souvenirs like Swiss watches, toys, and handmade crafts. The shops here have a cozy, old-fashioned feel.

- Zurich West

This part of the city has a more modern vibe with lots of trendy shops and boutiques. You can find stylish clothes, cool gadgets, and funky home decorations.

- Niederdorf

This is a lively area in the Old Town with lots of small shops and stalls. It's a good place to find gifts and local items. There are also many places to eat, so you can enjoy a meal after shopping.

- **Kreuzplatz**

This area has a mix of shops and is known for its variety. You can find everything from books and electronics to clothing and beauty products. It's a nice area to walk around and explore different stores.

Hotels (Accommodation Recommendations)

If you're looking for a hotel that offers a lot of comfort and extra services, Zurich has several great options. These hotels provide top-notch amenities and are located in convenient areas:

- **Hotel Baur Au Lac**

This is a high-end hotel located near Lake Zurich. It has beautiful rooms with great views and offers services like a spa, fine dining, and a fitness center. It's a perfect choice if you want a luxurious stay.

- The Dolder Grand

Another luxury hotel, The Dolder Grand, is known for its elegant design and excellent facilities. It has a large spa, a golf course, and fantastic views of the city and mountains. It's a bit farther from the center but worth it for the comfort and beauty.

- Hotel Glockenhof

Located in the city center, Hotel Glockenhof offers a mix of comfort and convenience. The rooms are modern, and the hotel is close to shopping areas and attractions. It also has a nice restaurant and good service.

- Hotel Zurichberg

This hotel is set in a peaceful area with a beautiful garden. It provides a relaxing atmosphere with modern rooms and offers a good restaurant. It's a short distance from the city center but offers a quieter stay.

Budget Options

If you're traveling on a budget, Zurich still has many affordable places to stay that are clean and comfortable:

- Ibis Zurich City West

This is a good option for budget travelers. The Ibis Zurich City West offers simple but comfortable rooms. It's located in a lively area with shops and restaurants and is easy to reach by public transportation.

- easyHotel Zurich

Another budget-friendly choice, easyHotel Zurich provides basic accommodations at a lower price. It's located a bit farther from the center but is well-connected by public transport.

- Youth Hostels

Zurich has several hostels that offer affordable rates. These are great for meeting other travelers and often have a fun, friendly atmosphere. They provide basic dormitory-style rooms and shared facilities.

- Hotel Marta

Located in the city center, Hotel Marta offers comfortable and affordable rooms. It's a good option if you want to be close to major attractions without spending too much. The hotel is simple but well-maintained and provides good value for money.

- Hotel Schweizerhof

For a mid-range option, Hotel Schweizerhof is reasonably priced and centrally located. It offers comfortable rooms and easy access to Zurich's main attractions and transport links.

Chapter Three: Geneva

Jet d'Eau (Key Attractions)

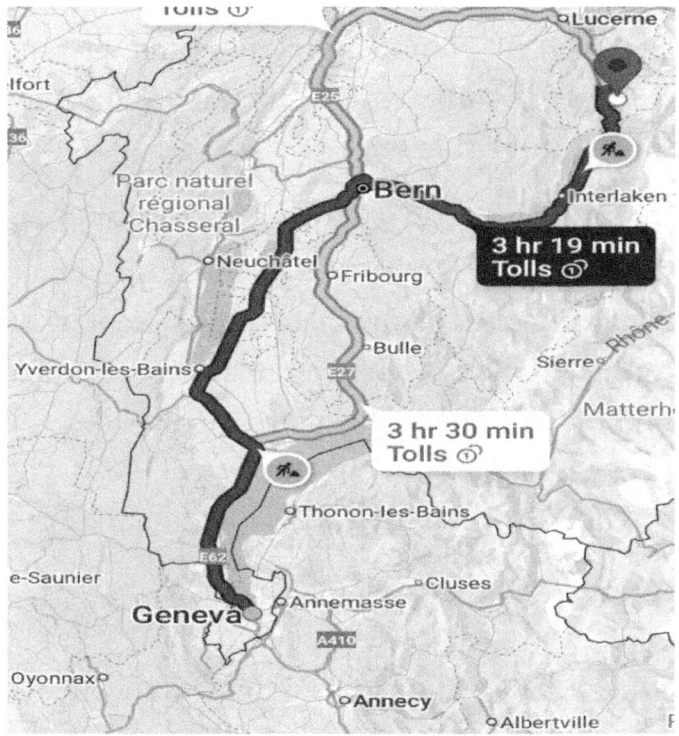

- The map above shows distance (with time covered) from Switzerland central area to Geneva

This is one of the most popular landmarks you can find in Geneva. It's a huge fountain located on Lake Geneva. The fountain shoots water high into the air, reaching up to 140 meters (about 460 feet). The Jet d'Eau can be seen from many parts of the city and is especially impressive when the sun makes the water sparkle.

The fountain was originally created to release pressure from a water pipe, but it became so popular that it was kept as a tourist attraction. It's a great spot to take photos and enjoy the view of the lake and surrounding mountains. If you get close, you might even get a little wet from the mist!

United Nations Headquarters

The United Nations Headquarters in Geneva is an important place where people from around the world come together to discuss global issues. The building is large and impressive, with beautiful gardens and flags from many countries.

You can take a guided tour of the United Nations Headquarters to learn more about its work and the important meetings that happen there. The tour includes visits to the Assembly Hall and the Council Chamber, where important decisions are made. It's a fascinating place to visit if you're interested in how countries work together to solve problems.

Geneva Old Town

Geneva Old Town is the historical center of the city. It's a charming area with narrow streets and old buildings. There, you'll find cozy cafes, small shops, and historic buildings.

One of the highlights in Old Town is St. Peter's Cathedral. This old church has been around for centuries and is known for its beautiful architecture. You can climb the tower for a fantastic view of Geneva and the surrounding area.

Another interesting spot in Old Town is the Maison Tavel, which is the oldest house in

Geneva. It has been turned into a museum that shows what life was like in Geneva a long time ago. You can see old furniture, tools, and learn about the city's history.

In Old Town, you can also visit the Place du Bourg-de-Four, which is a lively square surrounded by cafes and shops. It's a great place to sit, relax, and enjoy the atmosphere of the city.

Recommended Restaurants (Dining and Shopping)

Geneva has a wide variety of restaurants where you can enjoy tasty meals. Here are some restaurants in this area, which you can give a try to:

- Restaurant du Parc des Eaux-Vives

This restaurant is located near the park and offers a lovely view of the lake. The menu includes French and Swiss dishes, such as fondue and roast meat.

- Café du Soleil

Known for its traditional Swiss food, Café du Soleil is famous for its fondue and raclette. The cozy atmosphere makes it a perfect spot for enjoying classic Swiss dishes with family or friends.

- Bains des Pâquis

This restaurant is located on a pier and offers casual dining with a fantastic view of Lake Geneva. It's popular for its fresh salads, fish dishes, and the chance to enjoy a meal by the water.

- Les Armures

Located in Geneva's Old Town, Les Armures is known for its elegant setting and traditional Swiss cuisine. It's a good place to try Swiss specialties like raclette and rösti.

- L'Adresse

If you're looking for a modern dining experience, L'Adresse offers a mix of international and Swiss dishes. The restaurant has a stylish atmosphere and is great for a nice dinner out.

Boutique Shopping

When it comes to shopping, Geneva has some fantastic boutique stores where you can find unique and special items. Here are some top spots for boutique shopping:

- Rue du Rhône

In this place, you can find luxury brands and stylish clothing of any kind. It's a great place to look for something special or a high-quality souvenir.

- Carouge

Carouge is a charming area known for its artistic vibe and unique shops. The streets are filled with boutique stores selling everything from handmade jewelry to trendy clothes. It's also a lovely area to walk around and explore.

- Les Cygnes

Located near the lake, Les Cygnes is a boutique store that offers elegant clothing and accessories. It's a good place to find fashionable items and enjoy a pleasant shopping experience.

- La Halle de Rive

This shopping center is located by the lake and has a mix of boutiques and shops. You can find stylish clothes, accessories, and home goods. It's a great spot for a variety of shopping options.

- Antiquités - Au Vieux Genève

If you're interested in antiques, this shop offers a range of vintage items, including furniture and collectibles. It's a wonderful place to find a unique and historical piece.

Hotels (Accommodation Recommendations)

If you want a comfortable and high-quality stay, Geneva has several great hotels to choose from:

- Hotel Beau-Rivage

This luxury hotel is located right by Lake Geneva. It has beautiful rooms with stunning lake views and offers excellent service. You can enjoy fine dining in its restaurant and relax in a stylish setting.

- Hotel d'Angleterre

Another top choice for a luxurious stay, Hotel d'Angleterre is known for its elegant design and excellent location near the lake. The hotel provides high-end amenities, including a spa and gourmet dining.

- The Ritz-Carlton Hotel de la Paix

This hotel is located near the lake. It features well-appointed rooms, a spa, and several dining options. It's perfect for those who want a top-notch experience.

- Hotel Bristol

A bit more affordable than some luxury options, Hotel Bristol offers a comfortable stay with great service. It's centrally located, so you can easily explore the city and enjoy its attractions.

- Hotel Kipling Manotel

Located in the city center, Hotel Kipling Manotel is a good mid-range option. The rooms are modern and cozy, and the hotel is close to shopping areas and restaurants.

Budget Options

If you're traveling on a budget, Geneva also has many affordable places to stay that are clean and comfortable:

- Ibis Geneve Centre Nations

This hotel offers a good balance of comfort and price. It's located near the city center and provides simple, clean rooms.

It's a convenient option for those looking to stay in a central location without spending too much.

- Hotel St. Gervais

This budget-friendly hotel is located close to the city center and offers basic but comfortable accommodations.

It's a good choice if you want a place to sleep that is affordable and well-located.

- Geneva Hostel

For an even more budget-friendly option, the Geneva Hostel provides dormitory-style rooms at a low cost. It's a great place for meeting other travelers and is well-connected to the city's public transport.

- Hotel Auteuil

Located near the train station, Hotel Auteuil offers comfortable and affordable rooms. It's a practical choice if you need a place to stay that is close to transport links and city attractions.

- Hotel Astoria

This budget hotel is located near the train station and offers clean, simple rooms. It's a practical option for those looking for basic accommodations at a reasonable price.

Chapter Four: Lucerne and Lake Lucerne

Chapel Bridge and Water Tower (Key Attractions)

Chapel Bridge (Kapellbrücke) is one of the most famous landmarks in Lucerne. It's a covered wooden bridge that stretches across the Reuss River. The bridge was originally built in the 14th century and is known for its beautiful paintings that decorate the ceiling. These paintings show scenes from Lucerne's history.

The Water Tower (Wasserturm) stands next to Chapel Bridge and is part of the same complex. The tower was once used as a watchtower and a prison.

Today, it adds to the historical charm of the bridge. The combination of the bridge and the tower makes for a picturesque sight, especially when reflected in the water below.

Walking across Chapel Bridge is like stepping back in time. It's a great spot for taking photos and enjoying the view of the city and river. The bridge is often busy with tourists and locals, making it a lively place to visit.

Lion Monument

The Lion Monument (Löwendenkmal) is another important and moving attraction in Lucerne.

This monument is a sculpture of a dying lion carved into a rock face. It was created to honor Swiss soldiers who died while protecting the French King Louis XVI during the French Revolution.

The lion is shown with a sad expression, lying on its side with a broken spear beside it.

The monument is surrounded by a small park where you can sit and reflect. Many people find the Lion Monument touching and a powerful reminder of the bravery and sacrifice of those soldiers.

Lake Cruises

Lake Lucerne is a beautiful place to enjoy a boat cruise. The lake is surrounded by mountains and picturesque towns, making it a perfect setting for a relaxing boat ride. Here's what you can experience on a lake cruise:

- Scenic Views

As you cruise around Lake Lucerne, you'll see stunning views of the mountains and charming lakeside villages.

The clear blue water and lush green hills create a perfect backdrop for photos.

- Historical Boats

Some of the boats on Lake Lucerne are old-fashioned and add a touch of history to your cruise. You can enjoy a ride on these traditional boats while learning about the history of the area.

- Dining on the Water

Many boats offer dining options where you can enjoy a meal while cruising. This is a great way to experience the beauty of the lake and have a nice meal at the same time.

- Sightseeing Stops

Some cruises include stops at different towns around the lake, such as Weggis and Vitznau. These stops allow you to explore more of the region and enjoy the local culture and sights.

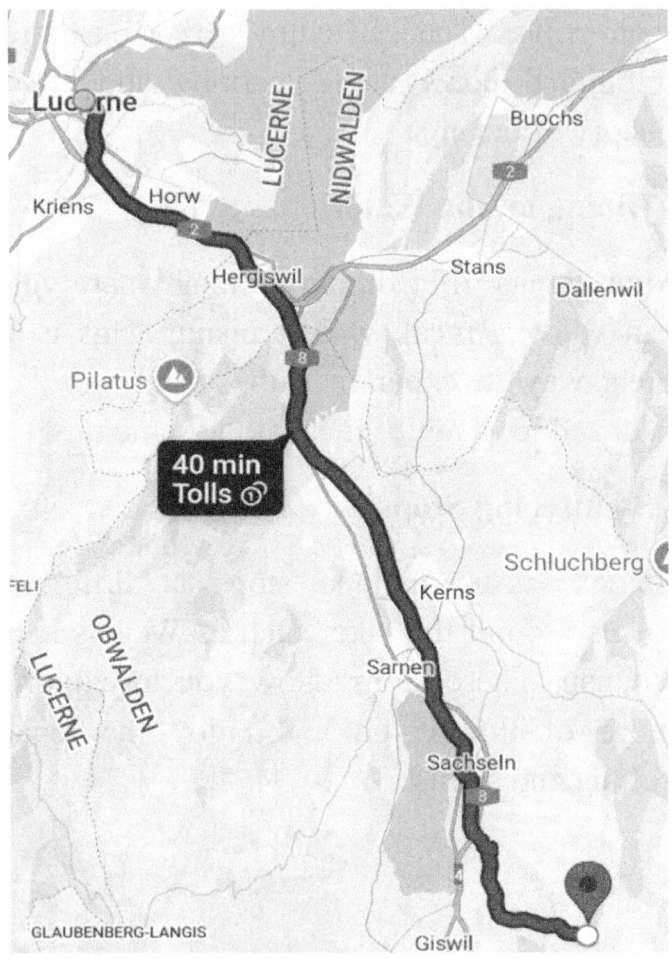

- The map above shows distance (with time covered) from Switzerland central area/location to Lucerne

Local Cuisine (Dining and Shopping)

When you visit Lucerne, you have the chance to taste some wonderful Swiss dishes. Some of them which you may need to try or consider are these:

- Rösti

Rösti is a tasty Swiss dish made from grated potatoes that are fried until crispy.

It's often served as a side dish with meals or topped with ingredients like cheese, eggs, or bacon.

- Fondue

Fondue is a fun way to eat melted cheese. You dip pieces of bread into a pot of melted cheese with a long fork. It's warm, gooey, and perfect for sharing with friends and family.

- **Raclette**

Raclette is another cheese dish that involves melting cheese and scraping it over potatoes, pickles, and vegetables. It's rich and delicious, especially on a cold day.

- **Swiss Chocolate**

This is common in Switzerland. You can find many types of chocolate, from creamy milk chocolate to rich dark chocolate.

- **Swiss Pastries**

You can enjoy various Swiss pastries, including buttery croissants and sweet cakes. These are perfect for a treat with a hot drink.

Shopping in Lucerne

Lucerne has some great places to shop, whether you're looking for unique items or just browsing. Here are some top spots for shopping in Lucerne:

- Old Town (Altstadt)

Lucerne's Old Town is a charming area with narrow streets and historic buildings.

Here, you'll find small shops selling unique souvenirs, local crafts, and Swiss gifts. It's a great place to pick up something special to remember your trip.

- Hofstrasse

This is a main shopping street in Lucerne with a mix of stores, including boutiques and larger shops.

You can find clothing, accessories, and other items here. It's a lively area with many options for shopping.

- Museggmauer (Musegg Wall)

The Musegg Wall is part of the old city walls and has some small shops and boutiques. It's a nice area to explore and discover unique items that you might not find in larger stores.

- Rosenburg Shopping Center

If you prefer indoor shopping, the Rosenburg Shopping Center offers a variety of stores, from clothing to electronics.

It's a convenient place to shop, especially if the weather isn't great.

- Werfthalle

Located near the lake, Werfthalle is a unique place that features a mix of shops and markets. You can find everything from local products to international goods. It's a good spot for discovering different types of merchandise.

Hotels (Accommodation Recommendations)

If you want a comfortable and upscale stay, Lucerne offers several great hotels:

- Hotel des Balances

This hotel is located in the heart of Lucerne, close to the main attractions. It has well-furnished rooms and offers good service.

The hotel is a short walk from places like Chapel Bridge and the Old Town, making it a convenient choice.

- Hotel Montana

Hotel Montana is known for its excellent location and beautiful views of Lake Lucerne. The rooms are modern and comfortable, and the hotel has a nice restaurant. It's a great choice if you want a mix of luxury and convenience.

- Hotel Vier Jahreszeiten

This hotel is a good option for those who want to be close to shopping areas and attractions. The hotel also provides good amenities and services.

- Hotel des Alpes

Located near the river and the Old Town, Hotel des Alpes is a comfortable hotel with friendly staff. It's a good place to stay if you want to be near popular sites and enjoy lovely views of the lake and mountains.

Budget Options

If you're traveling on a budget, there are several affordable places to stay in Lucerne:

- Ibis Budget Lucerne

This hotel offers simple and affordable rooms. It's located a bit outside the city center but is well-connected by public transport.

The hotel provides basic amenities, making it a practical choice for budget travelers.

- Hotel Fata Morgana

A budget-friendly option in Lucerne, Hotel Fata Morgana provides clean and simple rooms.

It's a bit farther from the city center but offers a good price for those who don't mind a short bus ride.

- Hotel Alpha

Hotel Alpha is another budget option that offers basic accommodations at a reasonable price. It's close to the train station and has easy access to the city's attractions.

- Youth Hostels

Lucerne has several hostels that are perfect for travelers looking for a cheap place to stay. These hostels offer dormitory-style rooms and a chance to meet other travelers. They are a good choice if you want to save money and enjoy a social atmosphere.

- Hotel Löwen

Located near the train station, Hotel Löwen is an affordable choice with comfortable rooms. It's a good option for those who need a convenient place to stay while exploring the city.

Chapter Five: Zermatt and the Matterhorn

Matterhorn Glacier Paradise (Key Attractions)

The Matterhorn Glacier Paradise is a fantastic place to visit if you love mountains and snow. It is the highest cable car station in Europe, located at 3,883 meters (12,739 feet) above sea level. To get there, you take a cable car ride from Zermatt that offers incredible views of the mountains.

At the Glacier Paradise, you can see the Matterhorn, which is one of the most famous mountains in the world. There is also an observation deck where you can look out over the Alps and enjoy a breathtaking panorama.

Inside, there's an ice palace with ice sculptures and tunnels made entirely of ice. It's a fun place to walk through and see the cool artwork. There is also a restaurant where you can enjoy a meal while taking in the beautiful mountain scenery.

Gornergrat Railway

The Gornergrat Railway is a historic train ride that takes you up to the Gornergrat ridge, offering some of the best views of the Swiss Alps. The train ride starts in Zermatt and climbs up to 3,089 meters (10,135 feet) above sea level.

The journey on the Gornergrat Railway is quite special because you pass through picturesque landscapes, including forests and meadows, and get amazing views of the Matterhorn and other surrounding peaks. At the top, you can enjoy a stunning view of the mountains and glaciers. There's also a restaurant and a souvenir shop where you can relax and buy a memento of your visit.

- **The map above shows distance (with time covered) from Switzerland central area to Zermatt**

Hiking Trails

If you enjoy hiking, Zermatt has some beautiful trails to explore. Here are a few popular ones:

- Five Lakes Walk (5-Seenweg)

This hike takes you past five mountain lakes, each with a different color. The trails are well-marked, and you get to see wonderful views of the Matterhorn reflected in the lakes.

The walk is about 9 kilometers (5.6 miles) and is suitable for families.

- Gornergrat Panorama Trail

This trail starts from the Gornergrat station and offers fantastic views of the surrounding mountains and glaciers. The hike is about 6 kilometers (3.7 miles) long and provides an opportunity to enjoy the alpine scenery up close.

- Matterhorn Glacier Trail

This trail gives you a chance to see the Matterhorn Glacier and the surrounding ice formations. It's a bit more challenging but offers spectacular views and a chance to experience the high-altitude environment.

- Sunnegga to Blauherd

This is an easier hike that takes you from Sunnegga to Blauherd.

Along the way, you get to enjoy beautiful views of the Matterhorn and the surrounding valleys. It's a great hike for families and those looking for a more relaxed walk.

Alpine Dining (Dining and Shopping)

When you're in Zermatt, trying some alpine dining is a must.

Alpine dining refers to enjoying meals in the beautiful mountain settings of the Alps.

Here are some top places to eat and what you can expect:

- Restaurant Chez Vrony

Located high up on the mountain, Restaurant Chez Vrony offers a fantastic view of the Matterhorn.

The restaurant serves Swiss dishes like fondue and raclette, which are perfect after a day of skiing or hiking.

The setting is cozy and the food is delicious, making it a great spot for a special meal.

- Restaurant Findlerhof

Another great alpine restaurant is Findlerhof. It's located in a picturesque area with views of the surrounding mountains.

They serve traditional Swiss food in a rustic setting. It's a wonderful place to try dishes like rösti and hearty mountain stews.

- Mountain Restaurant Rothorn

For a meal with a breathtaking view, the Mountain Restaurant Rothorn is a good choice. It's situated at the Rothorn peak and offers a variety of Swiss and international dishes. The large windows provide panoramic views of the Alps, making it a memorable dining experience.

- The Omnia Restaurant

This restaurant is part of the luxury Omnia Hotel. It's known for its high-quality cuisine and elegant atmosphere. The menu features a mix of Swiss and international dishes, and the food is beautifully presented. It's a nice place for a more refined dining experience.

Specialty Shops

In addition to great dining, Zermatt also has many specialty shops where you can find unique items.

Here are some interesting shops to visit:

- Chocolaterie Lindt

For those who love chocolate, the Lindt shop in Zermatt is a treat. You can find a variety of Swiss chocolates and sweets.

It's a great place to pick up gifts for friends and family or to enjoy a chocolatey treat yourself.

- Swiss Souvenir Shop

This shop offers a range of traditional Swiss souvenirs, including miniature Swiss watches, cowbells, and Swiss army knives. It's a perfect place to find something to remember your trip by.

- Zermatt Toy Store

If you're looking for something for children, the Zermatt Toy Store has a selection of toys and games. They also sell some Swiss-themed items that make great gifts for younger travelers.

- Alpine Fashion Boutique

For those interested in fashion, this boutique offers a selection of alpine clothing and accessories. You can find warm jackets, stylish hats, and other clothing items that are both practical and fashionable.

- Swiss Knife Shop

Known for its Swiss army knives, this shop also offers a variety of other tools and gadgets. It's a great place to buy a high-quality knife or multitool that can be useful for outdoor adventures.

Hotels (Accommodation Recommendations)

If you're looking for a comfortable and upscale place to stay, Zermatt has several nice hotels:

- Hotel Mont Cervin Palace

This hotel offers luxury and comfort with stunning views of the Matterhorn. It has spacious rooms and a range of amenities, including a spa and fine dining. It's perfect if you want a special experience and top-quality service.

- Hotel Alpenhof

Located near the center of Zermatt, Hotel Alpenhof provides a cozy and elegant atmosphere. The rooms are well-decorated, and the hotel offers excellent services, including a restaurant and wellness area. It's a good choice for a comfortable stay with easy access to the town.

- Hotel Zermatterhof

This is another luxury option with beautiful rooms and excellent service. It's close to the main attractions in Zermatt and has amenities like a spa and gourmet restaurant. It's ideal for those who want to enjoy a high-end experience.

- Hotel Bella Vista

Hotel Bella Vista has comfortable rooms and is conveniently located near the town center and ski lifts. It provides a good balance of comfort and value for money.

Budget Options

If you're traveling on a budget, there are also some great, affordable places to stay in Zermatt:

- Hotel Tannenhof

This is a budget-friendly hotel located a bit outside the main town area. It's a good choice if you're looking for basic accommodations without spending too much.

- Hotel Bahnhof

Located near the train station, Hotel Bahnhof provides basic and affordable rooms. It's a practical option for those who need a place to stay that's close to transport links and town amenities.

- Matterhorn Hostel

If you want to save even more, the Matterhorn Hostel offers dormitory-style rooms and private rooms at lower rates. It's a good place to meet other travelers and is well-situated for exploring Zermatt.

- Hotel La Ginabelle

This hotel offers budget-friendly rates while still providing a comfortable stay. It's located a short distance from the center of Zermatt and has simple but pleasant rooms.

- Guesthouse Murren

A bit farther from Zermatt, this guesthouse provides a more affordable stay with cozy rooms. It's a great option for those who don't mind a short trip to the main attractions.

Chapter Six: Interlaken, Bern, Lausanne, Montreux, St. Moritz, Vevey, and Sion

Key Attractions (Interlaken)

- Harder Kulm

Harder Kulm is a viewpoint that offers a great view of Interlaken and the surrounding mountains. To get there, you take a funicular ride up to the top. Once you reach the top, you can enjoy a panoramic view of the town, the lakes, and the peaks. There is also a restaurant where you can sit and enjoy the scenery.

- Trümmelbach Falls

These are impressive waterfalls located in a nearby valley. You can walk through tunnels and paths to get close to the waterfalls and see the water rushing through the rocky gorge. It's a fun and exciting way to experience nature up close.

- Schynige Platte

This is another great place to visit for amazing views. You take a cogwheel train up to Schynige Platte, where you can see beautiful views of the Jungfrau region and the surrounding mountains. There are also lovely walking paths and a flower garden.

- Lake Thun and Lake Brienz

Both lakes are beautiful and offer opportunities for boat trips. You can take a cruise to enjoy the scenery or just relax by the lakeside.

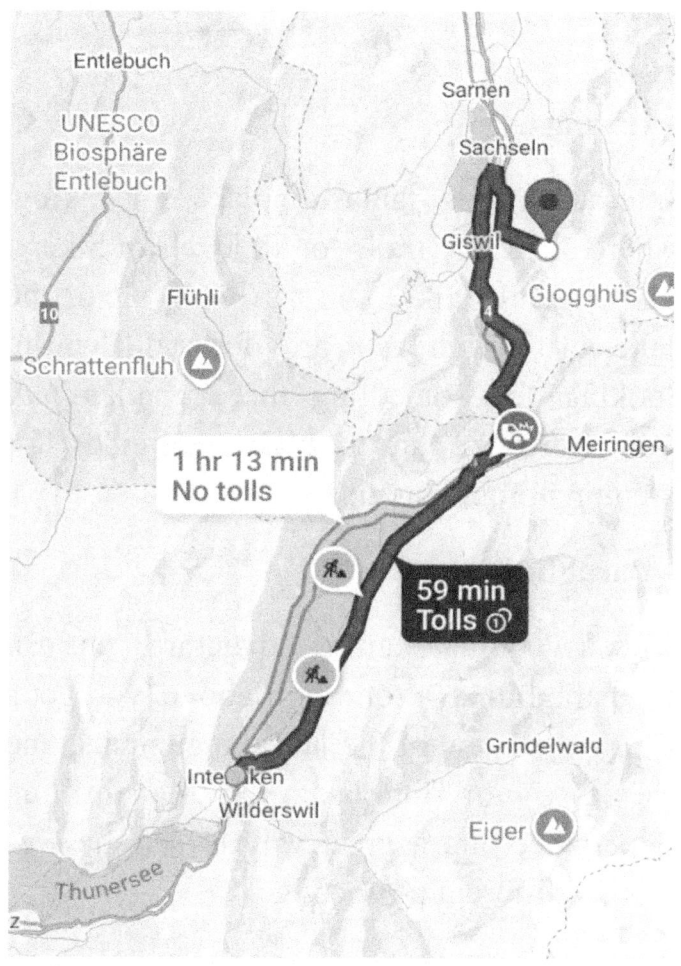

- The map above shows distance (with time covered) from Switzerland central area/location to Interlaken

Outdoor Activities

- Hiking

Interlaken is a fantastic place for hiking. There are many trails for all levels of hikers. For a gentle hike, you can walk along the lakes or through the nearby forests. If you're looking for something more challenging, you can hike up to higher altitudes for stunning mountain views.

- Paragliding

If you want an exciting adventure, you can try paragliding. From high above, you get a bird's-eye view of the lakes, mountains, and the town of Interlaken. It's a thrilling experience and a great way to see the area from a different perspective.

- Mountain Biking

Interlaken offers many mountain biking trails. You can ride through the forests and along the trails with beautiful views. There are options for both beginners and experienced riders, so everyone can enjoy a biking adventure.

- Canyoning

For those who love water adventures, canyoning is a fun activity where you climb, jump, and slide down natural water slides and waterfalls in the canyon. It's an exciting way to experience the rugged natural beauty of the area.

- Boat Rides

Taking a boat ride on Lake Thun or Lake Brienz is a relaxing way to enjoy the beauty of the lakes. You can choose from different types of boats, from quiet paddle boats to larger cruise boats.

Historical Sites (Bern)

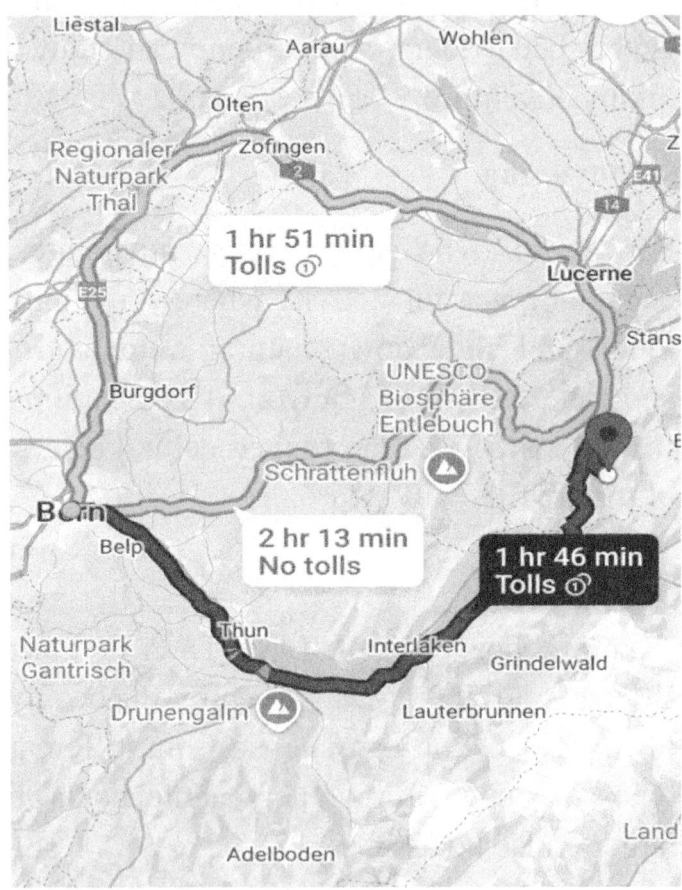

- The map above shows distance (with time covered) from Switzerland central area/location to Bern

- Zytglogge Clock Tower

In Bern, this is one of its most popular landmarks. This clock tower is very old and has a big clock that chimes every hour.

At the top of the hour, the clock puts on a show with moving figures and a trumpeting angel. It's a fun sight to see, and the tower has been part of Bern's history for hundreds of years.

- Bern Historical Museum

The Bern Historical Museum is a great place to learn about the history of Bern and Switzerland.

The museum has many interesting exhibits, including old objects, artworks, and historical documents. You can see how people lived in the past and discover stories about Bern's history. There's also a section about Albert Einstein, who lived in Bern for a time.

- Federal Palace (Bundeshaus)

The Federal Palace is the building where Switzerland's government meets. It is an important place in Bern and is located in the center of the city. You can take guided tours to learn about how the Swiss government works and see the beautiful rooms where decisions are made.

- Bear Park (BärenPark)

The Bear Park is a special place where you can see bears in a natural setting. The park is designed to look like the bears' natural habitat, and it's a fun way to learn about these animals. The park has been part of Bern's history because bears have long been a symbol of the city.

- Rosengarten (Rose Garden)

The Rosengarten is a lovely garden with many different kinds of roses. It also has a great view of the old town of Bern. The garden is a peaceful place to visit and learn about the city's history while enjoying the beautiful flowers.

- Einstein Museum

This museum is dedicated to Albert Einstein, who lived in Bern when he was a young scientist. The museum shows how Einstein's work changed the world. You can learn about his discoveries and see personal items that belonged to him.

- Gurten

The Gurten is a hill just outside Bern that offers a great view of the city and the surrounding area. It has been a popular spot for locals and visitors for many years. You can hike up the hill or take a funicular train to the top. Once you're there, you can enjoy the view and learn about the history of the area.

Museums (Lausanne)

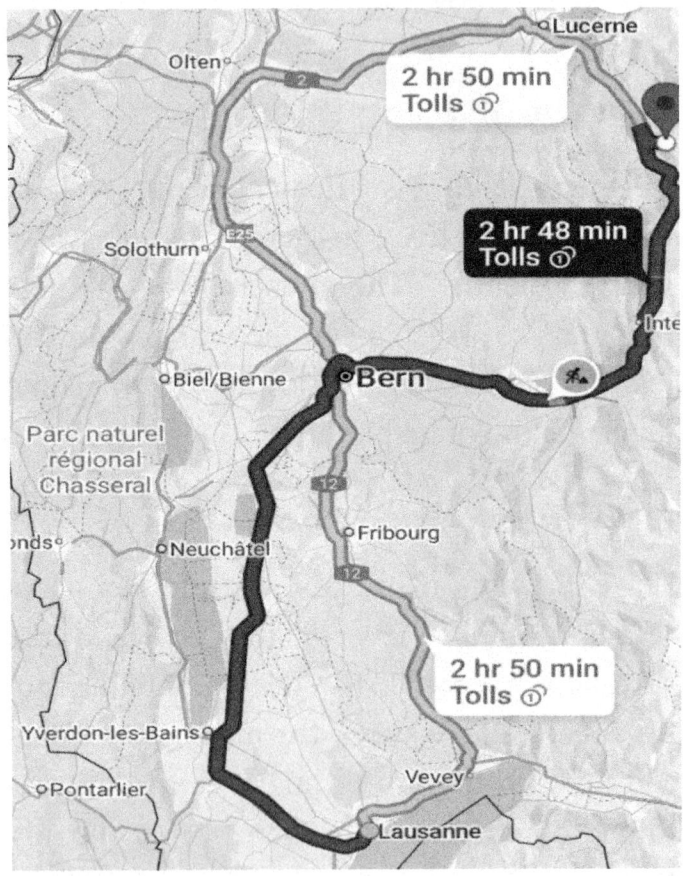

- The map above shows distance (with time covered) from Switzerland central area to Lausanne

- **Olympic Museum**

The Olympic Museum is one of the most famous museums in Lausanne. It's all about the Olympic Games and sports. You can see lots of interesting things, like old Olympic torches, medals, and uniforms. There are also interactive exhibits where you can try out different sports and learn about the history of the Games. The museum is located by Lake Geneva, and the view from there is really beautiful.

- **Collection de l'Art Brut**

This museum is dedicated to a unique type of art called "Art Brut," which means "raw art." This art is created by people who are not trained artists and often have their own special style. The museum has a big collection of these artworks, and visiting it is a great way to see something different and creative.

- **Musée Lausanne d'Histoire et d'Archéologie**

This museum, also known as the Museum of Lausanne History and Archaeology, is all about the history of Lausanne and the surrounding area.

You can see old artifacts, ancient tools, and learn about how people lived in the past. It's a great place to find out more about the local history and culture.

- **Musée de l'Élysée**

The Musée de l'Élysée is a museum dedicated to photography. It has a large collection of photographs from different times and places.

You can see famous photos and learn about the art of taking pictures. The museum also hosts exhibitions where you can see new and interesting work from photographers around the world.

- Musée des Beaux-Arts

The Musée des Beaux-Arts is an art museum with a wide range of artworks. You can see paintings, sculptures, and other art pieces from different periods and styles. The museum has works by both Swiss and international artists, and it's a great place to enjoy some beautiful and thought-provoking art.

- Musée Historique Lausanne

This museum focuses on the history of Lausanne and its people. It has displays about the city's past, including how it has changed over the years. You can see old maps, historical documents, and artifacts that tell the story of Lausanne from ancient times to the present day.

- Musée du Château d'Ouchy

Located in a beautiful castle by Lake Geneva, this museum is part of the Château d'Ouchy. It has exhibits about the history of the castle and its surroundings. The museum's setting is very picturesque, and it's a great place to learn about the area's history while enjoying the views.

Lakefront and Festivals (Montreux)

Montreux is a beautiful town in Switzerland located by Lake Geneva. It's known for its lovely lakefront and exciting festivals. If you're visiting Montreux, here are some key attractions you should check out:

• **Lakefront**

- Montreux Lakefront Promenade

The lakefront promenade in Montreux is a wonderful place to walk and enjoy the views. You can stroll along the path that runs beside Lake Geneva and see beautiful flowers, sculptures, and fountains. The area is perfect for a relaxing walk, where you can take in the fresh air and enjoy the picturesque scenery of the lake and the surrounding mountains.

- Chillon Castle

Just a short walk from Montreux, Chillon Castle is a must-see. It sits right on the edge of Lake Geneva and looks like it's floating on the water. You can explore the castle's rooms, towers, and ramparts, and learn about its history. The views from the castle are fantastic, and you can see the lake and the mountains in the distance.

- Montreux Rose Garden

Located near the lakefront, the Montreux Rose Garden is a beautiful spot where you can see many different kinds of roses. It's a colorful and peaceful place to visit, especially in the spring and summer when the roses are in full bloom. The garden also offers a great view of Lake Geneva and the mountains.

- **Festivals**

- **Montreux Jazz Festival**

One of the biggest and most famous events in Montreux is the Montreux Jazz Festival. This festival happens every summer and lasts for about two weeks. It features many different types of music, from jazz to rock and pop. You can see performances by famous musicians and enjoy live music in various venues around the town. The festival attracts people from all over the world and is a fun way to experience different kinds of music.

- **Montreux Noël (Christmas Market)**

In December, Montreux hosts a Christmas market called Montreux Noël. The market takes place along the lakefront and is filled with festive lights, decorations, and stalls selling holiday treats and gifts. You can enjoy hot drinks, pastries, and handmade crafts while soaking in the cheerful holiday atmosphere.

- Montreux Comedy Festival

This festival is dedicated to comedy and happens in November. It features performances by comedians from different countries. If you enjoy humor and want to see some great comedy acts, this festival is a fun event to attend.

- Montreux Jazz Artists in Residence

Besides the main jazz festival, Montreux also hosts special events with artists in residence throughout the year. These events give you a chance to see unique performances and workshops with musicians who are part of the jazz scene.

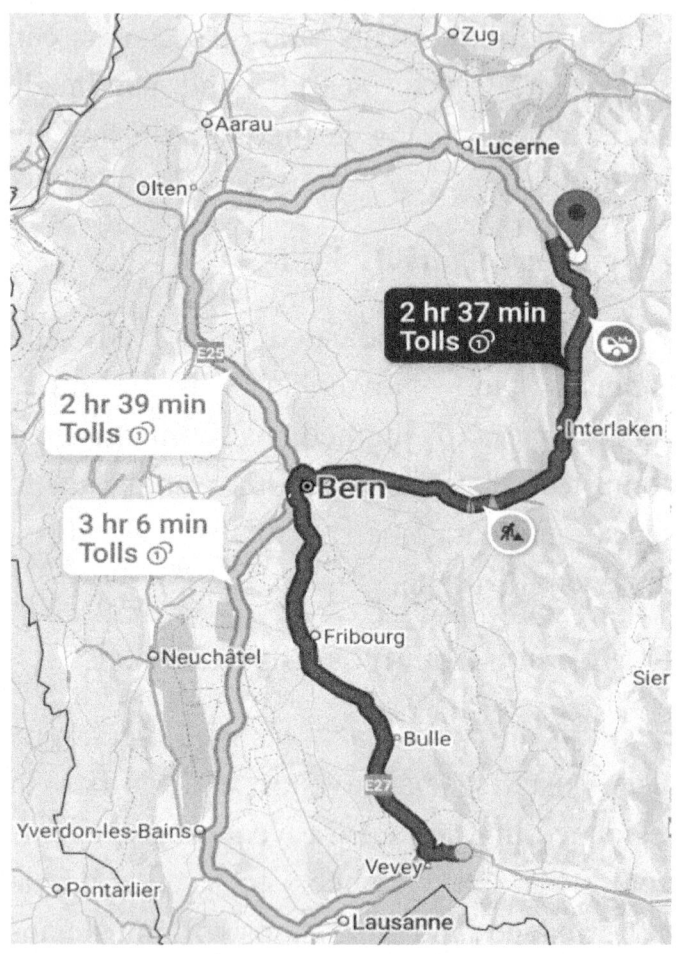

- The map above shows distance (with time covered) from Switzerland central area to Montreux

Winter Sports (St. Moritz)

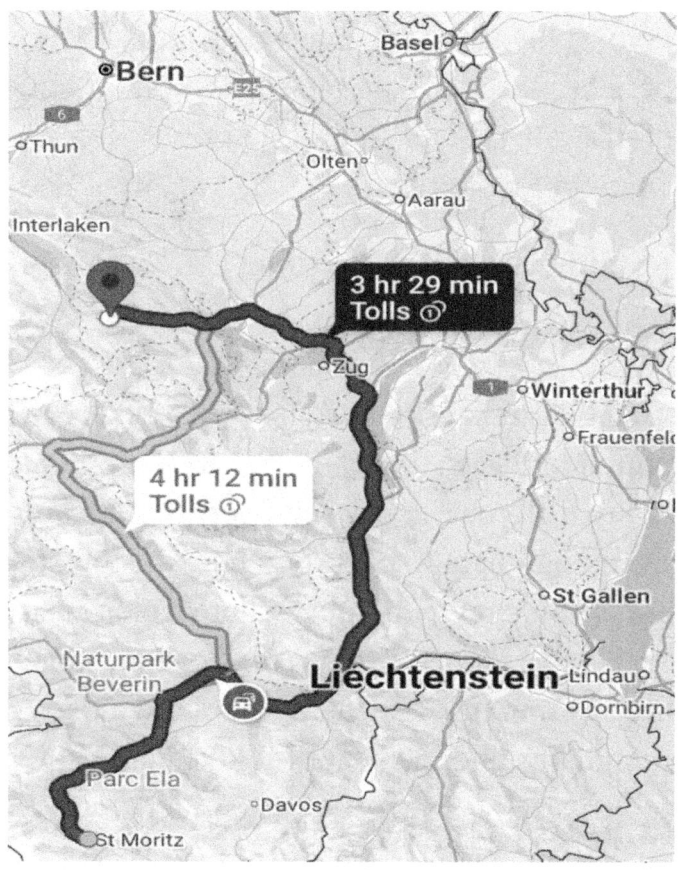

- The map above shows distance (with time covered) from Switzerland central area/location to St. Moritz

St. Moritz is a famous town in Switzerland known for its amazing winter sports. If you love snow and adventure, St. Moritz is a perfect place to visit. Here's a guide to some of the top winter sports activities you can enjoy in St. Moritz.

• **Skiing and Snowboarding**

- Corviglia Ski Area

The Corviglia ski area is one of the most popular places to ski in St. Moritz. It has many different slopes for skiers of all levels, from beginners to experts. There are also fun areas for snowboarding, where you can try tricks and jumps. The views from the slopes are stunning, with the snow-covered mountains and the beautiful lake below.

- Corvatsch Ski Area

Corvatsch is another great place for skiing and snowboarding. It has a large number of slopes and is known for having the longest ski run in the region. The area also has a fun park for snowboarders, with obstacles and jumps to challenge your skills. If you enjoy skiing at night, Corvatsch has night skiing on certain slopes.

- Diavolezza Ski Area

For those who like adventure, Diavolezza offers some exciting skiing options. The ski area is located at a higher altitude, which means the snow is often very good. The slopes here are a bit more challenging, making it a great spot for experienced skiers.

• Ice Skating

- Olympic Ice Rink

The Olympic Ice Rink in St. Moritz is a fantastic place to go ice skating. It's a large rink with a smooth, well-maintained surface. You can rent ice skates and enjoy skating around the rink. During the winter, the rink often hosts ice hockey games and figure skating events, so you might get to see some exciting performances.

- Natural Ice Rinks

St. Moritz is famous for its natural ice rinks on the frozen lakes. You can skate on Lake St. Moritz, which turns into a huge ice rink during the winter.

It's a unique experience to skate on natural ice with the stunning mountain scenery around you.

There are also ice hockey matches and curling games on the lakes, which can be fun to watch.

• **Snowshoeing and Winter Hiking**

- Snowshoe Trails

You can follow special trails that are set up for snowshoeing, which take you through beautiful snowy landscapes.

Snowshoeing is a fun way to explore the winter scenery at a slower pace.

- Winter Hiking Trails

St. Moritz has many winter hiking trails where you can enjoy a walk through the snow.

These trails are usually well-marked and take you through forests, meadows, and along the lakes. It's a peaceful way to enjoy the winter wonderland and take in the fresh mountain air.

- **Tobogganing**

- Preda-Bergün Toboggan Run

This is one of the longest toboggan runs in the world. You start at the top of a mountain and slide down a winding path all the way to the village of Bergün. It's a thrilling ride that's great for families and people who love a bit of excitement. The toboggan run is open during the winter season and is a fun way to enjoy the snow.

- **Bobsledding and Luge**

- St. Moritz-Celerina Olympic Bobrun

The Olympic Bobrun is a famous bobsled track that was used in the Winter Olympics. You can experience the thrill of bobsledding on this historic track, which is one of the few natural ice tracks in the world. It's an exciting adventure that lets you feel the rush of speed as you slide down the track.

- Luge Track

St. Moritz also has a luge track where you can ride on a small, single-person sled. The track is designed for both beginners and experienced lugers, and it's a great way to enjoy the speed and excitement of this winter sport.

Culinary Delights (Vevey)

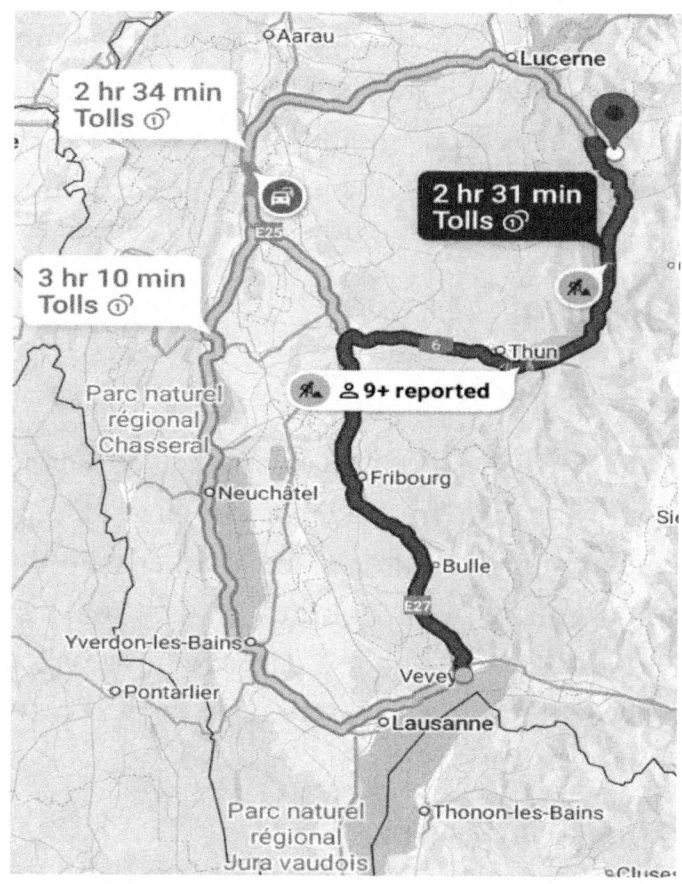

- The map above shows distance (with time covered) from Switzerland central area/location to Vevey

Vevey is a charming town in Switzerland known not only for its beautiful scenery but also for its delicious food. If you're visiting Vevey, there are some great culinary experiences you shouldn't miss. Here's a guide to some of the best places to enjoy food in Vevey.

• **Local Markets**

- **Vevey Market**

The Vevey Market is a lively place where you can find fresh, local produce. Every Tuesday and Saturday, the market fills the town square with colorful stalls. You can buy fruits, vegetables, cheeses, and baked goods. It's a great way to taste local flavors and see what's fresh and in season.

- **Montreux Market**

Although it's not far from Vevey, the Montreux Market is worth a visit. It has a variety of food stalls where you can find local specialties and treats. You can also enjoy freshly made meals and snacks while soaking in the vibrant atmosphere of the market.

• **Famous Food Spots**

- La Pinte Besson

This historic restaurant in Vevey is known for its traditional Swiss dishes. The menu includes classics like fondue and raclette, which are perfect for warming up on a chilly day. The restaurant has a cozy atmosphere and has been serving delicious food for many years.

- Les Trois Sifflets

Located in the heart of Vevey, this restaurant is famous for its creative dishes made from local ingredients.

They offer a mix of Swiss and French cuisine, with options like hearty stews and tasty pastries. It's a great spot to enjoy a special meal with family or friends.

- La Table du Baron

If you're looking for a more upscale dining experience, La Table du Baron offers a refined menu with elegant dishes. The restaurant focuses on using fresh, high-quality ingredients to create flavorful meals. It's a nice place to celebrate a special occasion or enjoy a memorable dining experience.

• Chocolates and Pastries

- Nestlé Factory Shop

Vevey is home to the famous Nestlé company, which is known for its chocolates and sweets. At the Nestlé Factory Shop, you can buy a variety of chocolate products and other treats made by the company. It's a fun place to explore and pick up some sweet souvenirs.

- **Confiserie Schmid**

This local confectionery is known for its delicious pastries and chocolates. You can find everything from creamy chocolates to delicate pastries. It's a wonderful place to enjoy a sweet treat or take home some tasty gifts.

• **Wine and Cheese**

- **Swiss Wine Cellars**

Vevey is in a region known for its excellent wines. There are several wine cellars in and around Vevey where you can taste local wines and learn about the winemaking process. Some cellars offer tours and tastings, making it a fun way to explore Swiss wine culture.

- **Cheese Shops**

Switzerland is famous for its cheese, and Vevey has several cheese shops where you can sample and buy different types of Swiss cheese. From creamy Gruyère to tangy Emmental, you can find a variety of cheeses to enjoy.

• **Culinary Events**

- Vevey Food Festival

If you're visiting Vevey in the summer, you might catch the Vevey Food Festival. This event celebrates local food and drink with stalls, cooking demonstrations, and tastings. It's a great way to try different dishes and experience the town's culinary scene.

- Cheese and Wine Events

Throughout the year, Vevey hosts special events focusing on cheese and wine. These events often include tastings, workshops, and presentations by experts. They are perfect for learning more about Swiss cheese and wine while enjoying some delicious samples.

Historical Sites (Sion)

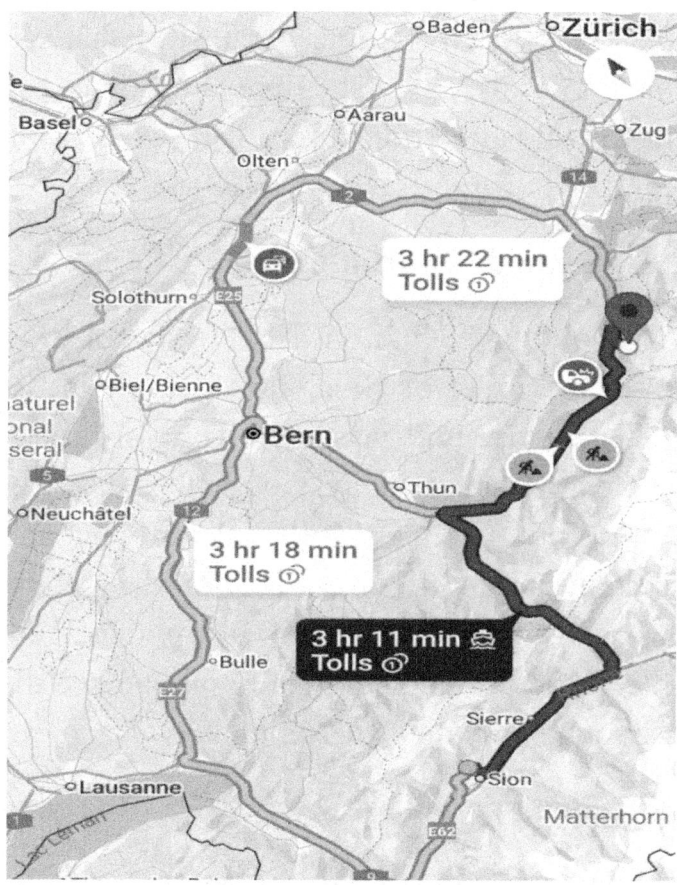

- The map above shows distance (with time covered) from Switzerland central area to Sion

Sion is a historic town in Switzerland with many interesting places to visit. If you love history, Sion has some great sites that tell the story of its past. Here are some key historical attractions you can explore in Sion:

• **Château de Tourbillon**

This old castle sits on a hill and looks out over the town of Sion. It was built in the 13th century and was used as a fortress to protect the area. Today, the castle is partly in ruins, but you can still walk around and imagine what life was like for the people who lived there long ago. The views from the castle are amazing, and you can see the surrounding valley and mountains.

• **Château de Valère**

Another impressive castle in Sion is the Château de Valère. This castle is even older than Château de Tourbillon, with parts of it dating back to the 11th century. It is also located on a hill and has a large, well-preserved church inside. The castle used to be an important place for religious ceremonies and is now a fascinating place to explore. From the castle, you can get a great view of Sion and the valley below.

• **Sion Old Town**

Walking through the old town of Sion is like taking a trip back in time. The streets are narrow and lined with old buildings that have been around for centuries. You can see historic houses, charming squares, and old churches. It's a wonderful place to walk around and enjoy the historical atmosphere.

• **St. Theodule Church**

This church is an important religious site in Sion. It has a long history and has been a place of worship for many centuries. The church has beautiful architecture and is known for its impressive interior. It's a peaceful place to visit and learn about the town's religious history.

• Sion Cathedral

The Cathedral of Sion, also known as the Cathedral of Our Lady of Sion, is a significant building in the town. It was built in the 13th century and has a beautiful Romanesque design. The cathedral's interior is just as impressive, with lovely stained glass windows and detailed stonework. It's a key part of Sion's history and is worth a visit.

• Musée d'Histoire de Sion

This museum is all about the history of Sion and the surrounding area. It has many exhibits that show how life in Sion has changed over the years. You can see old artifacts, maps, and displays that help you understand the town's past. It's a great place to learn more about the history of Sion.

- **Roman Ruins**

Sion has some ancient Roman ruins that you can visit. These ruins are from a time when the Romans lived in the area. You can see the remains of old buildings and streets that give you a glimpse into life during Roman times. It's a fascinating part of Sion's history.

Chapter Seven: 7-Day Itinerary

Day 1: Zurich

- **Morning: Arrival and Old Town Exploration**

When you arrive in Zurich, you'll start your day by discovering the charming Old Town.

The Old Town, or Altstadt, is like a big, open-air museum with its narrow streets and old buildings. Here, you can see buildings from many years ago that have been carefully preserved. As you walk around, you'll notice the old houses with their colorful facades and historic details.

A great place to start your visit is the Grossmünster church. This church is very old and has tall towers that you can climb to see a fantastic view of the city. It's a nice way to get a bird's-eye view of Zurich and see how the city spreads out below.

After visiting the Grossmünster, stroll along the Bahnhofstrasse, one of the world's most famous shopping streets. Even if you're not looking to shop, it's fun to walk along and see all the stylish stores and busy people.

Don't forget to explore the Lindenhof Hill. It's a peaceful spot that gives you a great view of the city and the river below. It's a perfect place to take a break and enjoy the view.

- **Afternoon: Lake Zurich and Bahnhofstrasse**

In the afternoon, head to Lake Zurich. The lake is beautiful and a great place to relax. You can take a leisurely walk along the lake's edge or even hop on a boat for a short cruise. The boat ride is a fun way to see the city from a different angle and enjoy the fresh air.

Near the lake is the Bahnhofstrasse, which is Zurich's main shopping street. Here, you can visit many shops, from big department stores to small boutiques. Even if you're not planning to buy anything, it's interesting to window-shop and see what's on offer.

There are also some nice places to stop for a snack or a drink if you need a break from walking.

- **Evening: Dinner and Local Entertainment**

Zurich has many great places to eat, so you'll have lots of options. You might want to try a local restaurant that serves Swiss dishes like fondue or raclette. These are traditional Swiss meals made with cheese that you melt and enjoy with bread or potatoes.

After dinner, you can experience some local entertainment. Zurich has a lively nightlife with many options for fun activities. You can catch a performance at one of the city's theaters, watch a movie at a local cinema, or visit a cozy café or bar to relax and listen to live music.

Another great option is to take an evening stroll around the city. Zurich's Old Town and lakefront are beautifully lit up at night, making for a pleasant and scenic walk. You might even come across some street performers or local events happening in the city.

Your first day in Zurich will be filled with exploring historic sites, enjoying the beautiful lake, and experiencing local dining and entertainment. It's a wonderful way to start your visit to this vibrant city.

Day 2: Lucerne

Morning: Travel to Lucerne and Chapel Bridge

Start your day with a journey to Lucerne, a charming city located by a beautiful lake. You can travel to Lucerne by train or car, enjoying the scenic views along the way. Once you arrive in Lucerne, your first stop will be the Chapel Bridge (Kapellbrücke).

The Chapel Bridge is one of the oldest wooden bridges in Europe and is very special. It was built in the 14th century and has a tower at one end. As you walk across the bridge, you'll notice beautiful paintings on the roof that tell stories from the past. The bridge stretches over the Reuss River and connects the two sides of the city. It's a lovely spot to take photos and enjoy the view of the river.

Next to the Chapel Bridge, you'll find the Water Tower. This old, round tower was once part of the city's defensive walls. It's a great place to learn about the history of Lucerne and see how the city was protected in the past.

- **Afternoon: Lion Monument and Lake Cruise**

After exploring the Chapel Bridge, head over to the Lion Monument (Löwendenkmal). This famous monument is a tribute to Swiss soldiers who died during the French Revolution. The statue shows a dying lion, and it's carved into a rock face.

It's very moving and a good place to learn about the history of Switzerland.

From the Lion Monument, make your way to Lake Lucerne for a relaxing cruise. The lake is surrounded by mountains and is a stunning place to enjoy a boat ride. You can choose from different boat tours that offer fantastic views of the lake and the surrounding scenery. As you cruise, you'll see charming villages, lush hills, and the beautiful Swiss landscape. It's a peaceful and enjoyable way to spend the afternoon.

- **Evening: Dinner in Lucerne**

In the evening, it's time to enjoy a delicious meal in Lucerne. The city has many wonderful restaurants where you can try local Swiss dishes. You might want to taste some classic Swiss food, like fondue, which is melted cheese enjoyed with bread, or raclette, which is cheese melted over potatoes and vegetables.

There are also many other types of food available in Lucerne, including Italian, French, and international cuisine. You can choose a restaurant with a nice view of the lake or a cozy spot in the city center.

After dinner, you might want to take a leisurely walk around the city. Lucerne is especially beautiful in the evening, with its lights reflecting off the lake and the charming streets lit up. It's a lovely way to end your day, taking in the peaceful evening atmosphere of this picturesque city.

Day 3: Interlaken

- **Morning: Travel to Interlaken**

Start your day by traveling to Interlaken, a beautiful town located between two stunning lakes, Lake Thun and Lake Brienz. If you're coming from Lucerne, the journey is quite scenic, with plenty of lovely views along the way. You can take a train, which offers a comfortable ride and lets you enjoy the Swiss countryside.

When you arrive in Interlaken, you'll see why it's such a special place. The town is surrounded by tall mountains and is known for its outdoor activities and beautiful landscapes.

• **Afternoon: Outdoor Activities and Lake Views**

After you get to Interlaken, it's time to enjoy some fun outdoor activities. Interlaken is famous for its adventures and is a great place to try something exciting. Depending on what you enjoy, you can choose from activities like:

- Paragliding

If you're feeling brave, paragliding offers an amazing way to see the town from above. You'll float through the air and get a bird's-eye view of the lakes and mountains.

It's a thrilling experience and gives you a different perspective of the stunning scenery.

- Hiking

For a more relaxed adventure, try one of the hiking trails around Interlaken. Some trails offer easy walks with beautiful views, while others are more challenging and provide breathtaking vistas of the lakes and mountains.

- Boat Ride

Another way to enjoy the lakes is by taking a boat ride. You can choose a boat tour on Lake Thun or Lake Brienz. The boat ride will let you see the crystal-clear water, charming lakeside villages, and the majestic mountains surrounding the lakes.

In the afternoon, you can also visit the Harder Kulm viewpoint. Take a funicular ride up to the top and you'll be treated to a fantastic view of Interlaken and the lakes below. The viewpoint is a great spot for taking photos and enjoying the beautiful scenery.

- **Evening: Relax and Explore Local Dining**

As the day winds down, it's time to relax and enjoy a meal in Interlaken. The town has many excellent restaurants where you can taste local Swiss cuisine or enjoy dishes from around the world.

- Swiss Cuisine

Try some traditional Swiss dishes like fondue or raclette. These dishes are made with melted cheese and are a fun way to experience Swiss food. You can find restaurants that serve these specialties in a cozy setting.

- International Food

If you're in the mood for something different, Interlaken also has restaurants offering Italian, Chinese, and other types of international cuisine. Whether you're in the mood for pizza, noodles, or something else, there's something for everyone.

After dinner, you might want to take a relaxing walk around town. Interlaken is lovely in the evening, with the lights reflecting off the lakes and the surrounding mountains. It's a peaceful way to end your day, enjoying the cool evening air and the beautiful surroundings.

Day 4: Zermatt

- **Morning: Travel to Zermatt**

Start your day by taking a scenic journey to Zermatt, a beautiful village in the Swiss Alps. The trip to Zermatt is like a moving picture show of nature. You'll see tall mountains, green valleys, and maybe even some cows grazing in the fields. The train ride is smooth and comfortable, and the views are simply amazing. As you get closer to Zermatt, you'll notice the famous Matterhorn mountain peeking through the clouds. It's a sight you won't forget!

- **Afternoon: Matterhorn Glacier Paradise**

Once you arrive in Zermatt, head straight to the Matterhorn Glacier Paradise. This place is known for its incredible views and fun activities. You'll take a cable car ride up to the glacier, which is like a giant ice park on top of the world. At the top, you can see the Matterhorn and other snowy peaks all around you. There's a snow park where you can play in the snow, and even a special viewing platform that feels like you're touching the sky. If you like adventure, you might also enjoy walking through an ice cave or trying out some cool slides. It's a fantastic way to spend your afternoon!

- **Evening: Alpine Dining**

As the day winds down, it's time to enjoy a cozy meal at one of Zermatt's charming alpine restaurants. Alpine dining is a special experience because it offers delicious, hearty food that warms you up after a day in the cold. You can try traditional Swiss dishes like fondue, which is melted cheese served with bread, or raclette, which is melted cheese poured over potatoes and vegetables. The restaurants in Zermatt often have a friendly, homey atmosphere, and you might even sit by a fireplace while you eat. It's a great way to relax and enjoy the evening after a day full of adventure.

Day 5: Geneva

- **Morning: Travel to Geneva**

Start your day with a train ride to Geneva, a beautiful city located by a large lake. The journey is smooth and gives you a chance to relax while enjoying the Swiss countryside. As you travel, you'll see rolling hills, green fields, and charming little towns. When you arrive in Geneva, you'll notice the lake right away—it's very big and looks like a sparkling blue blanket spread out before you.

- **Afternoon: Jet d'Eau and UN Headquarters**

After arriving, head to one of Geneva's most famous landmarks: the Jet d'Eau. This is a giant water fountain that shoots water high into the air, creating a spectacular sight. The fountain is so tall that it looks like a big, white plume rising up from the lake. It's a fun place to take photos and enjoy the fresh air.

Next, visit the United Nations Headquarters, which is not too far from the Jet d'Eau. This is an important building where people from different countries come together to talk about important issues and make decisions to help the world. You can take a tour of the building to learn more about how the UN works and see the large meeting rooms where important discussions take place. It's a great way to understand a bit more about world events and the efforts to keep peace.

- **Evening: Explore Old Town and Dinner**

As evening approaches, head to Geneva's Old Town, which is the oldest part of the city. The streets are narrow and winding, and the buildings have a lot of history. You can visit St. Pierre Cathedral, an old church that has been standing for centuries. Climb to the top of the cathedral for a fantastic view of the city.

After you're done exploring these amazing places, head over to a restaurant for dinner. There are many restaurants and cafes in this area where you can enjoy a meal. You might want to try some local Swiss dishes or simply enjoy a nice dinner with a view of the charming streets. The atmosphere is relaxed and friendly, perfect for ending a day of sightseeing in Geneva.

Day 6: Bern

• **Morning: Travel to Bern**

Begin your day with a train ride to Bern, the capital city of Switzerland. The journey is pleasant and gives you a chance to see more of Switzerland's lovely scenery. You'll pass by green fields, small villages, and beautiful mountains. As you get closer to Bern, you'll notice the city's unique charm. Bern is known for its historic buildings and friendly atmosphere.

• **Afternoon: Historical Sites and Bear Park**

Once you arrive in Bern, start by visiting some of its famous historical sites. The city's Old Town is a UNESCO World Heritage site, which means it's very special and has been preserved for many years. You can walk around the Old Town and see ancient buildings, old clock towers, and charming squares. One of the highlights is the Zytglogge, a clock tower with a big, impressive clock and moving figures that put on a little show every hour.

Another interesting place to visit is Bear Park. This park is home to several brown bears who live in a large, natural space where they can play and roam around. The park is designed to look like a real forest, so the bears have plenty of room to explore. It's fun and exciting to watch them play, and you can learn about their habits and the efforts to protect them.

• **Evening: Local Cuisine**

As the day turns into evening, it's time to enjoy a meal at one of Bern's local restaurants. The city has many great places to eat where you can try Swiss dishes and local specialties. Look for a restaurant that serves traditional Swiss food, such as fondue (melted cheese served with bread) or raclette (melted cheese over potatoes and vegetables). The food in Bern is hearty and delicious, perfect after a day of walking and sightseeing.

Enjoying a meal in Bern is also a chance to relax and soak up the local atmosphere. The restaurants often have a warm and cozy feeling, and you might even sit by a window to watch the city lights come on as the sun sets. It's a lovely way to end a day of discovering Bern's history and beauty.

Day 7: Lausanne and Montreux

- **Morning: Travel to Lausanne**

Start your day early with a journey to Lausanne, a beautiful city on the shores of Lake Geneva. Lausanne is known for its hills, stunning views, and charming streets.

If you're traveling by train, it will take about an hour to reach Lausanne from Bern, so make sure to grab a light breakfast before you leave. Once you arrive, you'll see that the city is full of life and interesting things to do.

- **Afternoon: Explore Lausanne and Travel to Montreux**

In the afternoon, explore some of the highlights of Lausanne. It's pretty good you begin with the Olympic Museum. Visit there and see things for yourself. This museum is not just about sports; it's also a fun place to learn about different cultures and the history of the Olympic Games. After that, head to the old town of Lausanne, which is full of lovely shops and cafes. The Cathedral of Notre-Dame is another must-see. It's an impressive building with great views of the city from its towers.

Once you've enjoyed your time in Lausanne, it's time to head to Montreux, which is about a 30-minute train ride away. Montreux is famous for its beautiful lakeside setting and charming atmosphere. You might want to have lunch before you leave Lausanne or enjoy a meal when you get to Montreux, as the journey will make you hungry!

- **Evening: Lakefront Stroll and Farewell Dinner**

When you arrive in Montreux, take a stroll along the lakeside promenade. This area is perfect for a relaxing walk with stunning views of Lake Geneva and the surrounding mountains. You'll find beautiful flowers, interesting sculptures, and plenty of spots to sit and enjoy the scenery.

As the evening comes, it's time for your farewell dinner. Montreux has many restaurants where you can enjoy a delicious meal while taking in the lake views. Try some local Swiss dishes or enjoy a meal with international flavors. It's a wonderful way to end your trip, reflecting on the amazing experiences you've had in Switzerland.

After dinner, you might want to take one last walk by the lake. The evening lights on the water are very peaceful and a perfect way to say goodbye to this beautiful country.

OTHER BOOKS RECOMMENDATION

Dear Reader,

If you liked this guide, **Jude** suggests checking out his other books, which you might want to add to your reading list.

Thank you for being a valued reader! He looks forward to accompanying you on many more literary journeys.

A KIND GESTURE

Dear Fellow Travelers,

Your feedback on the guide is important to **Jude**. If it made your **trip** more magical, he'd appreciate it if you left a review and shared your experience with others. By spreading the word, you'll help fellow travelers have amazing adventures too.

Thank you for being part of this community of great adventurers. Your kind gesture in leaving a review and recommending the guide is a meaningful contribution to the shared joy of exploration.

Safe travels and happy exploring!
Jude K. Bremner.

TRAVEL NOTE

TRAVEL NOTE

TRAVEL NOTE

TRAVEL NOTE

TRAVEL NOTE

TRAVEL NOTE

TRAVEL NOTE

TRAVEL NOTE

TRAVEL NOTE

TRAVEL NOTE

Printed in Dunstable, United Kingdom